Unlocking Your Purpose

By OD Harris

Unlocking Your Purpose
OD Harris
Copyright © 2015

Published in the United States by LuLu Press, Inc

3101 Hillsborough St, Raleigh, NC 27607

Library of Congress Cataloging-in-Publication Data

OD Harris

UnLocking Your Purpose

ISBN #: 978-1-329-40052-8
Editors

Tiffany C. Davis, Antoinette Halton-Singleton, Stanley Garland, Ed.S.

Printed in the United States

Cover Design: ED Hook senior consultant at Carefree I.T. Consultants

For you created my inmost being; you knitted me together in my mother's room.
I praise you because I am fearfully and wonderfully made;
your works are wonderful, I know that full well.
My frame was not hidden from you when I was made in the secret place.
When I was woven together in the depths of the earth,
your eyes saw my formed body.
All the days ordained for me were written in your book
before one of them came to be.

Psalms 139: 13-16

TABLE OF CONTENTS

Page

I would like to dedicate this book to every person that has made an impact in my natural and spiritual life. Special thank you to my Late Father, Ralph T Harris, my Mother Mozella Harris, and Siblings; My mentors Late Mother Elizabeth Singleton, Bishop Alfred Singleton Sr., Lady Antoinette Halton-Singleton, Bishop Alfred P. Singleton II, Lady Vivian Singleton, Pastor Tony & Barbra Brandon, Dr. Alfred Craig Sr. , Pastor Willie & Ruth Minor, Pastor Victor & Liz Trevino, Pastor John Hannah, Pastor Nancy P. Jones, Kim Milton-Mackey , Pam Leek, Mary Gibbs, The Bread House International Ministries, my good friends Pastor Ja'Meen Oliver, Alfred Singleton III, Shamar Flowers, Jecaro Flowers, Matt Moore, Leedon Jackson-Kelley.

God has a plan for your life.

Your part is to excavate the passion that will drive the purpose in fulfilling this plan.

INTRODUCTION

The professor briskly entered the room, walked quickly to his desk, and set his Starbucks coffee and his briefcase down; all the while scanning across the rows of desks to ensure they were all were occupied. He was not surprised as Humanities 101 was always packed with students who were quick to sign up for what they believed was an easy A. They would later realize their erroneous assumption.

The professor moved some papers aside as he sat on the edge of his desk. He scanned the sea of faces and asked, "Who are you?"

The student's faces immediately registered a look of confusion- as if to say *what, why don't you take attendance and then you will see who we are.*

He asked the question differently. "Does anyone here know who they are?"

A student sitting close to the door, his clothes rumpled and his hair uncombed, spoke lazily, "Sure I know who I am. I'm John Doe." Several students snickered at the response.

"No, wrong answer. You are not John Doe. That is who you are called. Your name is not who you are. Anyone else?"

A very pretty girl, sitting in the back, confidently stood up. "I am a beautiful, sexy female." This time everyone laughed, even the professor.

"No, wrong also. That is what you are; not who you are. Anyone else?" The class remained still.

The professor stood up and walked to the podium in front of the class. "Obviously, you all seem unable to answer such a simple question, let us begin Humanities 101, where you will learn just how difficult it is to peel away the layers of clan enculturation and discover who you really are. He slowly lifted his eyes and said, "And all of those looking for an easy A . . . this is your cue to leave."

CHAPTER 1

The Eternal Question: Who Are We?

As I was preparing my notes for this book, a friend of mine shared with me how her first day of school was, She walked in the classroom, went straight to the teacher, introduced herself and said, "I am an artist!" "Wow!" I responded. "At that young age?"

"Yes, I arrived on the planet knowing,. I always knew. Although, it is a wonder the artist in me survived as my parents did everything they could to cut any kind of non-conforming creativity from me."

Psychologists and human developmental theorists say that one's identity begins as soon as he or she exits their mother's womb. Identity is created in layers, the first being gender: *It's a girl! It's a boy!* The second layer of identity is applied once the newborn is named, oftentimes that name being of the father and/or grandfather's names if it is a boy, and the same for a girl with her mother's and/or grandmother's names . . *Elizabeth Rose Johnson* and *Robert Larry Stein,* for example, are names that have been handed down for generations.

By day three, the child is swaddled, carried home, and begins life within a familial/cultural clan, several generations old. (I refer to the term clan as representing the many layers of handed-down identities that are a part of a family's cultural history.) All aspects of that clan will mark the child's identity, perceptions, behaviors, and aspirations all the days of its life. Indeed, many human developmental theorists argue how the primary task of a growing individual is to separate itself from the stains of the familial clan. I believe that work begins almost immediately with *socialization.*

The Early Years: Conforming Behavior

What is your first memory of language? My friend, the artist, recalls her first memory: "I think I was around three years old. We lived in a big, old, Victorian house with a large hallway with darkly stained floors and the walls, were a soft crème color. I would lie on the floor and draw pictures on brown paper bags for hours. On one occasion, I simply ran out of room to draw, and being the logical creature that I was- I began drawing on the walls. Well, right in the middle of *my* pleasurable activity, I heard my mother shriek—a sound that I already knew very well. She quickly grabbed me up from the floor and as she switched me across the legs several times, as she screamed, 'NO! NO! NO!' The word no was very common to me in my household. Now as for the first time I heard the word yes, I have no such recollection, nor of hearing the words, great, wonderful, perfect, or awesome!"

Many of us were raised in very strict environments; perhaps many of you readers, like me, were raised in homes that were not child-proofed. Instead of freedom early on, you learned boundaries. As you stood by the coffee table; the colorful objects placed on that table were off-limits. You also learned grabbing items, other than your toys, could land you a quick swat on your hand. This was considered to be a time when parents actually *parented* and young children learned appropriate behavior.

I remember once, when I was around four, sneaking into the kitchen to touch the stove. My mother had insisted that I not be in the kitchen because the stove was hot. Perhaps it was because I had no idea what hot really meant, and sure enough, my curiosity got the best of me. Needless to say, I slipped past her and touched the stove and yes, the stove was hot and I burned my finger. To make matters worse, I could not ask my mother for medicine, because she would know I had disobeyed her and I would be in even more trouble. Children are vulnerable in their curiosity and eagerness to explore. They are also vulnerable to the *tales* of things that can happen to them. Once at a Thanksgiving feast, my father told me to be careful while I was eating watermelon. He said, if I swallowed a seed, a watermelon patch would grow in my belly. Now, why my father would tell me such a thing, I don't to this day know, however, I believed what he said. Rest assured the day came when I *did* swallow a watermelon seed and that night, I was sure that the pains in my stomach were because vines were growing in my belly. For years, I was very careful to pluck the seeds out of any slice of watermelon I was about to eat. Really, I still wonder the purpose of telling a child such a thing?

On the other hand, a parent's behavior can leave a comforting impact on a child's life that will last all of their days. My minister father often left impressions that are very sacred to me. I remember one very stormy night. Heavy wind was lashing rain against the windows. Thunder seemed to crash down right on top of our house, and lightning cracked across our lawn in jagged bolts of whiteness. I was so scared I could not sleep, so I ran to huddle with my sisters. As the storm even grew fiercer, my father got up from his bed, and walked into the living room. He stretched out his hands and rebuked the winds to calm down and commanded the rain to fall gently. He simply said, "Peace, be still." And, the elements of nature listened. I felt so protected by my father. I remember thinking to myself, "I want to be just like him." It would be many years later that I would realize the lesson in this experience: When one has a deeply rooted character born of an absolute belief in something, it is a powerful currency by which one can create change.

I was a child of the familial clan and my rearing and punishment came mostly from my older relatives. My family structure was hierarchal, based on age. I was taught to respect all the elders of my family even if they were teenagers. My older sister and my older cousin were in charge of me once, and neither of them hesitated to spank me whenever I did not do as I was told. This dynamic was the created lens by which I viewed approval; in my mind, everything was *yes* and *no*, what I could do and what I was not allowed to do. Most situations were very black and white, not a lot of grey. The apostolic faith of my family and the strict doctrine of what was acceptable offered very narrow defined opportunities. We went to church so much, and the teachings of our faith were so slanted towards negating so many life experiences that would be considered "fun," such as dancing or going to the movies, it would take years to unpack the layers of familial/religious identity that had been embedded in my childhood

11

psyche.

Not to say my identity was some terrible state of condition. It was not. In actuality, it was a normal state as we are all products of our early familial and cultural environment, which in turn is determined by the circumstances of the times. We, all of us, are informed by our clan. Our job becomes one of discrimination—what aspects of our childhood indoctrination do we want to keep, and which ones do we find irrelevant and desire to let go of.

A Positive Experience of Identity Imprinting

Rae-Ireland, my artist friend who I mentioned earlier, created a great example of a positive identity imprint when she quickly informed her first-grade teacher, not only who she was, but also what she was: "I am an artist!" That's a remarkable bit of self-knowledge that most kids do not have by the first day of school. Even more remarkable, it seems her identity as an artist was already firmly established that day. This allowed her to skip some of her classes and decorate the hall bulletin boards, and in third grade, she was selected from all the students in her school to work with the art teacher to prepare paper maché instruments to decorate the auditorium for the state's symphony performance. Subsequently, there were many first place ribbons for the PTA art contests. Rae-Ireland remembers throughout middle-school and high school, there were many times when she felt inadequate, judged, and intimidated. During those times her identity as an artist gave her the strength to push forward, ignoring the immediate environment that was not very supportive.

I think her early identity imprint was unusual. Most kids in early grade school have a sense of what they like and what they don't like, and that's about it aside from their clan imprinting.

How About You?

Can you think of an early memory when you realized you had a talent or quality that was solely yours within your family clan? When did you first realize some of your unique talents or qualities that set you apart as an individual within your family? How did this knowledge strengthen you and serve you during your early school years? How are those talents and qualities manifested in your life today?

CHAPTER 2

The Need to Challenge: The Preadolescent Years

Once a child enters school, it is his or her task to become a good little duck and waddle in the same manner as all the other little ducks through the lock-step system of early education. Most children are a conforming animal by this time, with a thorough set of yesses and no's, do's and don'ts. They know their name and who their clan is. Things go rather well during this time.

As preadolescents entering middle-school, however, things quickly change. Preadolescence is an exciting time of change and challenge, although this is often a confusing time for them as well. The process of identity ideation is just around the corner, generally arriving around the ages of eight to ten. Identity ideation is a time when children begin to realize a concept of "self" that is separate from their identity as a member of a familial clan. During this time, a child shows a greater sense of self-identity and increased feelings of independence usually emerge as the child begins to view him or herself as an individual, and not simply as just one of the family clan.

In the process of ideation, preadolescents begin to discover self-dimensions, such as their personal attributes, their preferred activities, ways in which they are different from family members and schoolmates, and personal traits and attitudes.[1] This is a time when preadolescents begin developing the abilities to reason, which grants them the ability to take on the perspectives of others. Suddenly, they may question the beliefs they have been raised with, and they wonder about their self-identity with regards to beliefs that they question as being correct and/or appropriate. They begin to see the flaws in authoritative figures, especially regarding their parents; hence, this is a time when a

---

[1] Marcia, J. E., (1966). Development and validation of ego identity status, *Journal of Personality and Social Psychology*.

different view on morality might surface. New pictures of themselves emerge and the opinions of their parents can be quiet different from those of their friends, whose views and opinions now hold a great deal if persuasive power. I was definitely impacted by my own realization of the social incongruence of my familial belief systems with those of my friends. I was raised as a strict Christian. We were not allowed to go to the movies, an activity that I personally never thought was wrong, although many Christians of our faith rallied against the unsavory, sinful environment a movie theatre *supposedly* fostered. To me, a movie was simply a movie and nothing else. As one might expect, in my teens I rebelled against this type of thinking and went to the movies anyway. We were also taught not to play cards or dance. Anytime we did something that was not aligned with our brand of the Christian faith, they were considered in rebellion against God and the behavior was a sure-fire ticket to hell.

From my early years of clan indoctrination, I grew up thinking the very definition of hell was being disobedient. We were so focused on sin; I think we missed the merciful part of God's grace. I was defined by the standards the familial clan had set for me. In my ideation years, I began to seriously question some of the constraints of our particular brand of faith. By high school, I rebelled and decided I would make my own decisions leading to how I would be defined. I learned in this process if one does not take time to explore, analyze, and evaluate the familial belief systems that have heretofore defined them, others will be quick to determine who and what you are . . . in their terms, of course.

One of my friends told me his experience with the ideation process created a major conflict with his father. His father was a heavy drinker, causing several issues within the family. He was also very prejudiced, especially towards Blacks, Jews, and Catholics. During the seventh grade, my friend got an afterschool job with one of the families on his block. The Martins lived in a very large house with a beautiful yard, full of flowers, and small sculptures. My friend was to work every Saturday mowing their lawn, trimming the shrubs, and cutting away any dead flowers.

1

He found the family to be wonderful to be around and he looked forward to spending his Saturdays with them.

One day, Mr. Martin told him he would not be needed for the coming Saturday as the family had a christening to attend and afterwards, there would be a celebratory luncheon at the home. He asked my friend if perhaps he could come on Friday after school; if that were possible, and for the change, he would pay him extra. During the conversation Mr. Martin just happened to mention that Catholic christenings always meant there would be a lot of relatives present, so he and his wife had decided to have an outdoor luncheon. My friend was surprised and asked Mr. Martin if he and his family were Catholic. Mr. Martin looked at him strangely and replied, "Yes, is that an issue for you?" My friend was very embarrassed and answered, "Absolutely not, it's just that I've never met a Catholic person before and I think your family is wonderful. I love my time spent here!" While walking home, my friend found that he was growing angrier by the minute at the nonsense his father had been spewing about Catholics. How "Catholics are ruining the country, and that there will probably be one in the White House before long." I am sure his father had worse things to say about the Jews, as he called them collectively. The idea popped into my friend's head that his father had probably never even met a Catholic or a Jew. Furthermore, if Catholics were as nice as Mr. Martin and his family, then he would sign up! Catholics must have been doing something right--their family was certainly nicer than his. Once he arrived home, he told his father that Mr. Martin was a Catholic; consequently, his father demanded that he could no longer return to "that house" again.

My friend refused to obey his father's demand, as he had experienced Mr. Martin as being one of the nicest people he had ever met, and he refused to be prejudiced against people because of their religion or their race. The outcome of this experience for my friend was what developed a heightened sense of advocacy for the underdog and an advocacy for the identification of discrimination. As he grew older, he had a zero tolerance for the discrimination practices. For the rest of his father's life, he remained at odds with him.

This is a perfect example of how individual ideation will often separate preadolescent self-reflection and self-determination from the imprinting of the familial clan. Ideas that lead to discrimination are usually deeply embedded in a family's belief systems. It takes a brave stand to break away from such beliefs. On the other hand, many children often mimic their parents' beliefs well into adulthood, unless some kind of catalyst for change occurs, those individuals will take their parents' belief systems with them to their grave; never once challenging validity. Worse still, they will pass these same beliefs on.

Impression Management and Self-Presentation

Behavioral theorists Thomas Brinthaupt and Richard Lipka consider the ideation process as one of "impression management" and "self-presentation" as pre-adolescents struggle with self-consciousness, introspection, inner conflict, and uncertainty regarding their
place in the greater scheme of things, peer pressure, school-related anxiety and competition.[2] Obviously, this is a critical time for good parenting and those children that are well supported in the midst of identity ideation will move through this stage of development with a greater sense of self-worth and self-knowledge as to what they are capable of achieving. Those children who do not have a positive support system tend to experience self-esteem issues that arise daily with lower self-worth outcomes, increased vulnerability to depression, and lower intrinsic motivation. Moreover, as previously mentioned, those children whose parents have imprinted them with hateful ideologies will suffer through middle school with critical self-esteem issues that often manifest in violence by the time they are young adults.

17

Pre-adolescents do not sit on a fence well. If the familial clan beliefs are not in harmony with the beliefs children experience in school environments, the child will feel compelled to choose one over the other. This is a time when they drop the notions of becoming Spiderman or Princess Bella and latch onto more realistic work expectations, such as being an astronaut, a doctor, a horse trainer, etc. They also develop their own ideas regarding morality, fair play, and right versus wrong.

This is also an exciting time of exportation and discovery for the child who has developed a strong sense of personal identity and capability and feels well supported by peers and other-adults (these would be teachers, counselors, coaches, etc.). It is a time for budding painters, guitar maestros, phenomenal athletes, and emerging scholars. Successful middle schools provide a nurturing environment where the exploration and development of many "possible selves" is supported. This is part of the ideation process as pre-adolescents learn they are multi-dimensional beings, whereas in their early childhood, this was not even a cognitive concept.

During my middle school years I explored many areas of interest. I tried sports, but they just weren't my thing. I switched my focus to music and tried playing the violin in the school orchestra. I quickly discovered I didn't like the violin, so I switched to the trombone and found that I liked it very much. I also tried other extracurricular activities, such as participating in a talent show reciting a psalm that my Mother had written, but none of these activities seem to really resonate with me. This type of exploration is what all middle schools should be fostering [as these years are a critical time for exploratory activities within a safe and nurturing environment—activities which are centered on successful ideation concepts, unconnected to scholastic achievement].

---

[2] Another interesting aspect of pre-adolescent ideation is children will often develop a sense of intention to do and become something, which they will act upon with a great deal of persistence. They gain a newly developed sense they can do something that will have an effect for the greater whole. Brinthaupt, T., & Lipka, R. (Eds.) (2002). Understanding early adolescent self and identity: An introduction. NY: SunyPress

It is equally important that outcomes of exploration be *recognized*. I remember in the sixth grade, I made the momentous decision to run for student leadership. I did not win the presidency; however, I did win a seat on the leadership council based on how well I managed my campaign. One promotion the leadership council supported was a canned food drive. Students were to bring in a few canned goods from home. The classroom that brought in the most can goods would win a prize—a certificate, a merit medal, or a celebratory dinner. I think my competitive nature and my desire to do well had to compel me to go door-to-door to collect canned goods. I ultimately collected more than one hundred cans for my classroom. In fact, I was so driven to succeed; I used a baby stroller having only three wheels to do my collecting. The principal and faculty felt that I had gone beyond the call of duty and I was honored with a certificate, a merit award, and dinner! The greater result of my effort was that my classmates also began collecting in their neighborhoods. By the end of the drive, we had collected more than 300 canned goods for our class. What seemed a little disappointing at the time was that a girl classmate, Kiowa Roper, beat me. In reality, she empowered my competitiveness. My remaining middle school years, I continued to collect door-to-door during the food drive, which culminated in my collecting 635 canned goods for my eighth-grade class. I seemed driven to raise the bar each year, but more for my own self-satisfaction than for school recognition. I realized the collecting of canned goods and the distribution to the poor was a significant activity that affected everyone in a positive manner. Through this experience, I realized how I enjoyed helping others who were in need. I felt a real passion for it. I also learned that while I *did* want to be considered cool by my peers, I wanted to be useful in helping the needy *more*. I realized if given an idea to follow, I could successfully execute it and produce a successful outcome. Thus, a big chunk of my self-identify was formed during these ideation years. I didn't realize at the time, I had reached a cornerstone of my life purpose.

CHAPTER 3

The High School Years: A Worldly Awareness

While the middle school years are a time to form an identity separate from the familial clan, the high school years say; now that I know who I am, what am I supposed to do with this knowledge? In other words, now that I am an individual separate from my family, what part do I, as an individual, play on the world stage?

Unfortunately, the education system in the U. S. doesn't fully prepare students to answer such questions. Rather, the focus or push it is to continue to higher education, which to me, is somewhat of an oxymoron. Current statistics reveal that 50-70% of students changed their major an average of three times over the course of a four-year degree. It is not rocket science to realize twelve years of mandated schooling has not sufficiently educated our children to the degree that they have a formidable cache of self-knowledge. Without that knowledge, how are they supposed to envision their place in the world as adults? How are they supposed to uncover their purpose?

Renowned educator Sir Ken Robinson, PhD, internationally recognized leader in the educational development of creative, imaginative, and innovational programs for school systems, makes the case for the necessity of finding one's passion as it will be sorely needed in carving out a worthy life pursuit. His 2006 TED Conference talk regarding talent, creativity, innovation, and passion is the most viewed in TED's history--more than 25 million times, and has been seen by an estimated 250 million people in over 150 countries. In his book, "Finding Your Element: How to Discover Your Talents and

Passions and Transform Your Life," he writes, "All children start their school careers with sparkling imaginations, fertile minds, and a willingness to take risks with what they think. Most students never get to explore the full range of their abilities and interests . . . Education is the system that's supposed to develop our natural abilities and enable us to make our way in the world."[3] Research suggests the priority concern for high school students is how they are going to make their way in the world. The lucky ones have had good role models to emulate while growing up. Others have had such terrible adult models in their life that, while they might not know much about personal passion, they certainly know what they don't want to become. There are the many students who move about as unknowns, searching for *some* kind of identity and purpose in life.

I was a lucky one. In high school, I continued my participation with the student council and leadership within the school ranks. I still continued in music because that made me happy. Things were going well for me and then, in the space of a few moments of realization, my spirit was broken. On that day, I had spent an afternoon at the birthday party of my oldest nephew. When I returned home, I found my father on the porch sitting in his favorite porch rocker; he had passed from this world. I was crushed. For many days and nights, I locked myself in my room and cried. In the early mornings, I could hear the agonizing cries of my mother downstairs. Our home had a huge empty space in it and we struggled mightily to get through. I clung to my father's words that I had heard in his sermons many times: *Grace be to God who is the keeper of peace.* When I needed it most, God was there to comfort me.

My father was a good man. He had a good heart and loved his family. His love had few boundaries, which allowed him to minister to people all the time. His unselfishly labored and well-earned legacy imprinted many people with a map on how to live a purposeful and meaningful life. As the months passed and routine once again settled in, I spent a lot of time considering the philosophical implications of life . . . its possibilities, its meanings, its unique heartbeat and I realized how short of an experience life really is. It seemed to me that a quality pursuit of one's time ought to mean something, so when our unique heartbeat stops beating; one can look at their life experience and think, *well done!*

After my father died, I became more active in school and church programs. On one level, it was a way to spend time hiding from pain. There were many days that I felt discouraged, but I believed in the power of self-motivation and in positive self-talk when I needed encouragement. On another level, and one I'm sure my father would have approved, my becoming more involved in helping other people was a way for me to move forward.

In death, as in life, my father continued to keep a strong, guiding, and loving, hand on my back. In time, I looked to my pastor as a father figure, and while my mother had always been one of my hero's, I felt like I needed a man to guide me. The men in my church family began playing a significant role in my development.

I have always had a distinct awareness of the role that inherent faith had in my life. My pastor's living example was crucial to my understanding of the grace of faith. He taught a real man serves God! Another minister who played and continues to play a very impacting role in my life is Minister Tony Brandon. I came to know Minister Tony and his wife, Barbara, when he invited some of the young, fatherless boys (and there were lots of us in our community) to play basketball with him after school. Before long, this youth ministry grew from a backyard family gathering to a community-mentoring program (which later won a state award for its anti-violence, anti-gang message, and its positive influence on youth).

Minister Tony was very strict. He allowed no profanity or "trash talk." He had a clear vision of what he wanted to accomplish with the motley crew of mostly fatherless kids in his community. He also knew what it would take to create "leaders of tomorrow." It was his intention to seed ideas of community advocacy and self-responsibility and he was intent on tending that garden. Such was his intent that it forged a very high expectation of manly behavior. Although there were times when I stumbled, and Minister Tony never hesitated to tell me when I was wrong,

---

[3] Robinson, K. (2013). Finding your element: How to discover your talents and passions and transform your life. Viking: USA.

I would strive to excel in his eyes, as I knew he loved me [as one of his own and I could not disappoint him]. He never judged me by my mistakes and rarely reminded me of any improper past behavior by saying, "OD, I have already told you . . . ." The most valuable advice this man gave me as a growing teen was to follow my heart and "never make excuses . . . a man always owns his decisions." Minister Tony tremendously shaped me. He recognized my talents, my desire to lead, and he raised me to the status of a leader. After a while, I was no longer the mentored; I became the mentor. I became the one the other kids looked up to. Minister Tony began to groom me as a motivational public speaker and I loved it. I wasn't quite sure how my service would all come about, but it was during this time that I faintly recognized a slight dimension of what my purpose might become.

Another aspect of my high school experience that dovetailed nicely with my nascent sense of purpose was my recruitment into the ROTC in the tenth grade. I decided to join ROTC partly to honor my dad and partly in a search for my individual identity. Through the activities and structure of the ROTC, I learned discipline and how to focus my energy to stay with a project to its completion. I also became more socially conscious as I was involved with many community outreach events, such as community beautification projects, collecting food for the homeless, and visiting the elderly to give assistance in things they were no longer able to do.

Amidst it all, I still struggled with lack . . . the lack of knowing who I was and what I was meant to do with the life given to me. I graduated in the top 5% of my class. I played in the high school band. I played basketball on a winning team. I was an honor student. I struggled with a lack of direction for my life and my career. I remember my pastor preaching a sermon titled, *Walking Your Purpose*, and all I could think about was the lack of connection I had to my purpose. I knew what I was good at and what I enjoyed doing, and what I felt passion for, but this knowledge was useless without direction coupled with a strong desire to be successful. Although I knew what my talents were, I didn't have a clue as to what to do with them.

A man's gift makes room for him.
Proverbs 18: 16

Every experience I had from childhood to high school had formed my perceptions of who I was. In my early childhood years, my family defined who I was. During my middle school years, as my self-awareness developed, I recognized that I had several dimensions beyond the narrow definition of my family. I began to think out of the family circle and come up with ideas of my own about how things should be. It was in my high school years that I came to understand what I could become with hard work and dedication. Even then, I still was not my own individual as I carried a strong clan identity. What if I had rebelled against my early socialization and against my upbringing? What if, contrary to everything that had defined me, I chose a different path, alienated the identity given to me by others? How accepted would I have been then? In these years of individual mental growth, I realized that we often must break away from the herd and go exploring the fields by ourselves. There is nothing quite like alone-time to simply think about the meaning and relevance of all the things you think about. That is the truest path to self knowledge.

The Error of Premature Identity Foreclosure

James Marcia, a prominent psychologist whose work has focused extensively on the adolescent-psychosocial development and lifespan development, cautions on the consequences of what he terms *identity foreclosure,* which is when a commitment is made without exploring alternatives. As previously talked about, many times commitments are based on parental ideals and beliefs that are accepted without question. As Marcia explains it, ". . . the individual about to become a Methodist, Republican farmer like his Methodist, Republican farmer father, with little or no thought in the matter, certainly cannot be said to have "achieved" an identity, in spite of his commitment."[4]

24

Adolescents may foreclose on a handed-down familial clan identity willingly or under pressure. Dependent on the family clan dynamic, a *negative-identity* occurs when an adolescent adopts an identity in direct opposition to that which is expected, just like my friend experienced with his narrow-minded father and his Catholic neighbor. Although my friend would never consider his decision to split with the clan perspective a negative-identity experience, he was an exceptionally strong-minded person, a trait that has worked well in his favor throughout his adult life. He has never regretted breaking away from his father's beliefs in lieu of his own.

The flip side of the parent-child identity dynamic (and there is always a flip side) was, for me, the influence of my father's career experience. His career ups and downs, have more than anything, influenced my own career decisions. My father was laid off from his factory job several times. I saw first-hand how demeaning it was for him that someone else held the power to determine the amount of financial security he could provide for his family. The factory seesaw style of labor kept my parents from getting ahead and prospering. I realized during my middle-school years that we were socially poor. This was a very uncomfortable realization. Economically, we had adequate housing, food, and clothing, and we had lovely home, amazing holidays, and sometimes vacations.

Nevertheless, the late 80s and most of the 90s were a time of prosperity for Americans . . . with equal time for electronic gadget/games consumption. One of those games that I badly wanted was a Gameboy. That was not to be though, as our family lived in adequacy rather than social consumption.

---

[4] Marcia, J. E., (1966). Development and validation of ego identity status. *Journal of Personality and Social Psychology*.

I'm sure there were many families like ours as this was the era when factories began phasing out human workers in lieu of robotics. I learned two important lessons during this time—one, what it felt like to be on the fringes of having those things I desired but could not afford, and two, the individual power that resided within the business model. These realizations, more than any other, forged my decision to attend college and major in business. I entered college six months after I graduated high school, with my quilted patches of self-identity and a determination to become successful in a career where I could have some control over its direction and outcome.

Think about some of the philosophies handed down to you by the familial clan that you have held onto without questioning. Have they defined you, empowered you, or held you back?

Chapter 4

Your Generational Identity

For I know the plans I have for you, declares the Lord, plans to prosper you
and not to harm you, plans to give you hope and a future.

Jeremiah 29:11

By the time an individual has navigated the often-murky waters of higher education, that individual has earned a new layer of identity, courtesy of modern sociologists. They are a Gen X, a Gen Y, or a Gen Z, depending on their birth date (Gen-XersGen-Xers are those born between 1965 and 1980). These new identities are loaded with carefully researched historical and demographic descriptions, which bode rather well for the Gen-XersGen-Xers -- not quite so well for the Gen Ys and Gen Zs. (I remained curious what the next Gen will be after Z). Generation X is a tag that was actually coined by the famous photographer Robert Capa in the early 1950s. He used it as a title for a photo- essay about young men and women growing up immediately after the Second World War. The term really took off in 1991 when Douglas Coupland's novel, *Generation X: Tales for an Accelerated Culture*, a work that focused on the lifestyles of young adults during the late 1980s, was released. Soon thereafter ad agencies used the tag to refer to a distinct population for marketing purposes.

Gen-Xers were identified as laid back, market savvy, considerably imprinted with mass media and MTV, and the first generation of "latchkey" kids that were exposed to lots of daycare time and divorced parents. They were also labeled as the generation with the lowest voting participation rate of any previous generation. Newsweek described them as "the generation that dropped out without ever turning on the news or tuning in to the social issues around them." Gen-Xers were also often characterized as having high levels of skepticism and a "what's in it for me" attitude. That said, Gen-Xers are arguably the best educated generation with a third obtaining a bachelor's degree or higher.

27

Now that the Gen-Xers have grown into full adulthood, the layers of identity that have been fostered upon them have changed over the last few years. In her book, *Generation X Goes Global: Mapping a Youth Culture in Motion*, Professor Christine Henseler describes Gen-Xers as "a generation whose worldview is based on change, on the need to combat corruption, dictatorships, abuse, AIDS, a generation in search of human dignity and individual freedom, the need for stability, love, tolerance, and human rights for all."[5] According to authors Michael Hais and Morley Winograd, There's been a shift in the status of the Gen-Xers, who are now looked upon as an "idealist generation" that has encouraged individual enterprise and business risk-taking, where customers and their needs have become the North Star for an entire new generation of entrepreneurs.[6] Yet, the most shocking aspect of the Gen X identity is the new description of also being a Gen Flux, which refers to the recent phenomenon of making several career changes throughout one's lifetime of employment. The days of being "a company man" are considered over, as globalization has created a chaotic job market. This identity is also applied to the Gen-Yers.

The Gen-Yers are those born between 1980 and 2000, about 71 million of them which now range in age 14 to 34. Gen-Yers (also called the Millennials) are known as incredibly tech-savvy, and more racially and ethnically diverse. They are a hard lot for ad agencies to crack as they are fairly immune to traditional marketing. Sales pitches need to be innovative and fast-moving to capture their short attention-span. They have few loyalties to brand names and are quick to experiment with change, especially with regards to fashion. They are savvy shoppers—one in nine has their own credit card, co-signed by a parent. The majority of Gen-Yers have been raised in dual income or single parent families. Many sociologists have long-considered Gen-Yers as, in a word, *spoiled*. Researchers tend to agree as they have found that Gen-Yers have been pampered, nurtured, and programmed with a slew of activities since they were toddlers, meaning

---

[5] Henseler, C. (2012). Generation X goes global: Mapping a youth culture in motion. NY: Routledge
[6] Winograd, M., & Hais, M. (2012). Why Generation X is sparking a renaissance in entrepreneurship. *Inkadescent—Ezine for Entrepreneurs.*

they are both high-performance and high-maintenance, according to author Bruce Tulgan, founder of Rainmaker Thinking.[7] The millenniums are the most child-centered generation ever and their expectations for their lives are different. They are independent and financially smart, and as far as work goes, they place a higher value on self-fulfillment, than on a specific career. They want jobs with flexibility, telecommuting, and family-time options. According to Tulgan, this is a generation of multitaskers; they can read e-mails while talking on their smart phones while trolling online. "They're like Generation X on steroids," Tulgan says. "They walk in with high expectations for themselves, their employer, and their boss."

At the high end of the Gen-Yers, individuals are making considerable inroads in changing corporate concepts and they find working in a global environment stimulating. They are fearless in the workplace. For many, they found their passions early and they have pursued their multiple purposes with laser intensity. On the low end, the youngest Gen-Yers are out of work. Many have recently obtained university degrees with enormous student-loans attached to them, most in the thousands of dollars. It has been said that this is the first generation of graduates to finished college bankrupt. These young millenniums have lost faith in most everything that holds our society together— politics, commerce, religion, and especially the idea that higher education will provide meaningful employment--once considered a sure path to a successful life.
Many continue to live with their parents while they take low-wage jobs for which they are well over qualified, accept part-time work at minimum wage, and tackle the necessary evil of the unpaid internship . . . a new corporate incentive that allows the student to build "valuable experience," while the company, of course, benefits from free labor in innovation and vision. The promise of the Internet flooding the world with employment opportunities has been anti-climactic as Internet businesses offer opportunities for labor and services with wages that are well below minimum. Take for example, the many sites that offer positions for writers . . .

---

[7] Tlgan, B. (2009). Not everyone gets a trophy: Managing Generation Y. MA: Jossey-Bass.

for example, the average eLance writing assignments pay $1.00 an article, others sites pay as much as 3¢ a page. In spite of being better educated, more accomplished, and more tech savvy than any previous generation, Gen-Yers have the economic decks stacked against them. They did everything right to obtain the holy grail of success, as prescribed by previous generations; yet, somewhere mid-stream, the rules changed to their disadvantage. Statistics show that 53% of recent grads are jobless or underemployed. Twice as many grads are in minimum wage jobs as compared to five years ago, and to make matters even more severe, student debt has topped the $1 trillion mark. Is it any wonder that the young Gen-Yers are demoralized, cynical, hopeless, and depressed?

A New Social Phenomenon: The Emerging Adult

Incredibly, sociologists have emerged with a new term for the predicament young Gen-Yers are in, which according to Jeffrey Arnett of Clark University, is a distinct stage of life--the "emerging adulthood." A New York Times magazine feature summarized the current patterns for young Gen-Yers: Across the United States, twenty-somethings are taking longer to finish school, leave home, begin a career, get married and reach the other milestones of traditional adulthood.[8] In addition, Dr. Arnett argues that this new life stage has certain key characteristics, such as identity exploration, self-reflection and self-focusing, feeling untethered and lost, and remarkably a continued belief in possibilities and opportunities.

Apparently the 20s brain is still evolving and will continue to do so until an individual is in his or her thirties. Neuroscientist Jay Giedd at the National Institute of Mental Health argues that the 20s-something individual is wise to postpone some of life's major decisions as it makes sense biologically. "The 20s are really a time for self-discovery . . . it allows individuals to adapt to changing environments. We can figure out what kind of world we live in and what we need to be good at."[9]

---

[8] Arnett, J. (2004). Emerging adulthood: The winding road from the late teens through the twenties. MA: Clark University.
[9] Jabr, F. (2012). The neuroscience of 20-somethings. *Scientific American.*

Developmental psychologist, Lawrence Steinberg of Temple University, agrees and suggests " . . . [in this stage] there's better communication between parts of the brain that process emotions and social information—like what people think of you—and the parts that are important for planning ahead and balancing risk and reward."[10]

There is some good news in this new research. It seems the emerging adulthood stage comes with some special brain capabilities that offer enormous opportunities. First is the opportunity to passionately and uninhibitedly go after big goals, figure out life's big questions, and make important commitments. Second, is the opportunity to take an active role in the development of the executive part of your brain in order to create a foundation for lasting success.

In light of the latest research on human development, when I consider my views upon entering college, I have to ask myself the question: What was I thinking??

Led Astray by the Big Lie

Honestly, I was thinking to "fit in." I was thinking about becoming a responsible, college-educated adult. I was thinking about creating success for myself. I did not approach college with the idea of exploration. Actually, that concept never entered my mind as I felt at the time that anyone planning to attend college, and willing to make the financial sacrifice to do so, should surely have a plan—and that plan certainly needed some kind of vision regarding its outcome. And why shouldn't I, and millions of other brainwashed students, have believed that we were making the right choice . . . the only choice that would guarantee a career over a job, and success over a mediocrity? Beginning in middle school, we had been reminded at every turn that a college education was an absolute necessity for achieving personal and financial success. Most of our parents were baby-boomers and an extended (a Masters and a PhD) academic career had worked quite well for them. It seems that no one foresaw (other than Bob Dylan, were they even looking?) that the times were indeed "a'changing."

We Gen-Xers were a focused lot, for the most part, and with a slight degree of snobbishness, held strongly to the notion that our college education would open career doors immediately upon our graduation. More than a few of us were in for a devastating shock. It wasn't long before our thinking changed and we no longer referred to *our careers* or our *career goals* as these had no place to exist. The doors were, not only, not opening to welcome us into corporate affluence; but many were sealed shut to our shouts of earned entitlement and the bombardment of our professionally polished resumes. The new employment currency became a *job* and soon enough that changed to *any job.*

Many of us were slapped with disappointment and disillusionment as we realized that we had been told a big lie by the system that had institutionalized us for sixteen years, and then some. We were simply gullible cogs in a huge machination called higher education. The outcome wasn't their problem; it was ours.

It's a devastating, gutting realization to come to terms with the fact that after doing, and doing well I might add, all the prescribed tasks for success, the affluent career and its financial rewards are not waiting on the threshold as you ascend from the steps, after picking up your MBA diploma. It doesn't take long before another realization hits you head on—you need a job, and soon thereafter, your perspective changes even more, and it's no longer *a* job that you're after, it's *any* job . . . any honest job that is offered to you. The notion of *your life's purpose* has long since flown the coop. What is now taken its place are menial jobs like dishwashing, being a janitor, working at Goodwill, stocking grocery shelves . . . all at minimum wage. Is it any wonder that the discovery of *real life* for the Gen-Xers and Gen-Yers has been so depressing?

CR

The Gen-ZersGen-Zers: A Completely Different Paradigm

Our Future: Will they know who they are and what they are capable of?

The very youngest Generation is the Gen-ZersGen-Zers, born between the years of 1995 and 2012. Their current numbers are 23 million and growing. These individuals, by the virtue of being born in a technologically driven society, will change the world with their highly developed tech capabilities and Star War visions. Schools will become the most

diverse they have ever been as higher technological capabilities will drive innovation and change. It is difficult to even imagine what this generation will have accomplished by the time they are in their mid-adult years. For the Gen-Zers, the concept of individual passion and purpose may hold more promise than the previous generations of the Xers and Yers. Our world is so complicated, its societal issues so grave, its major economies in such dire straits, and its political systems so damaged and riddled with greed. The Gen-Zers will surely have to find a different kind of ground to stand on while they wage a battle against failing systems, and a call to arms by a multitude of like-thinkers to create a new world order. If any cause ever needed invested passion and purpose, it will be the causes embraced by the Gen-Zers. My hope is that their light and fire will not be extinguished by their despair and disillusionment about what currently seems to be a broken, unsalvageable world. The key for the Gen-Zers lies in their securing an individual purpose, driven by an enduring passion. How difficult that will be is yet to be determined.

Chapter 5

The Quest for Purpose

It isn't normal to know what we want. It is a rare and difficult psychological achievement.

Abraham Maslow, Humanistic Psychologist

Nearly everyone has some knowledge of Maslow's hierarchy of needs, which is often illustrated as a 5-layered pyramid with the largest, most fundamental level of needs at the bottom, and the supreme need for self-actualization at the top.[11] Maslow argued that every person has a strong desire to realize the full potential of his or her intellectual capabilities and creative talents. However, it's the trip from the most basic level of providing for one's needs to the apex of self-actualization that is the rare and difficult achievement. It is akin to the knight-errant finding the Holy Grail. That medieval quest is as relevant today as it was a thousand years ago.

Quest is an interesting word that conjures up images of vast areas of desolate desert terrain to be crossed, or miles of rugged mountain terrain to be climbed, or mighty seas to be conquered. We generally think of the extraordinary occurring during such feats of solitude and physical endurance. Yet, the true meaning of the word quest has little relationship to the notion of overcoming heroic obstacles of mental and physical endurance. Quest, in its 14th century medieval French origin, *queste*, referred to a pursuit of inquiry. It is the forerunner to the word *question*. In actuality, the Holy Grail is symbolic of the pursuit of self-actualization. The vast, arduous terrain of our quest lies within each of us. Our capabilities and talents are like jewels. They are our non-renewable natural resources that are buried deep within our physical caverns. We honestly don't know what these resources are until we deliberately engage in a quest to

---

[10] Maslow, Abraham. (1998). Toward a psychology of being. (3rd ed.) NY: Wiley, 1998.

discover them. When we do, we find God's own life-sustaining clay, waiting for us to mold it into the fully actualized person we were meant to be.

In my experience, most people respond to the idea of a quest in search of their talents and capabilities as ridiculous at best, and a colossal waste of time in more lukewarm terms. I think the problem is that individuals simply have no idea of where or how to look for their inherent resources. My grandfather used to say, "God doesn't send you into the world without a suitcase and a roadmap." I think this is true. The difficulty is, many of us have lost the key to unlock our resources and have forgotten how to read the map.

To a significantly large degree, we have accepted our great educational system, which continually strives to steer its students away from self-knowledge. This system is concerned with developing good little workers for our corporations, financial institutions, and government entities. At what point in our education does the realization hit us that we are ill-equipped to travel with our God-given suitcase and roadmap? For most, it is when we frame and hang our higher education diplomas and ask, now what?

> *Understand that an eagle never flies without a purpose*
> *and a dog never bites without a reason.*
>
> O.D. Harris

So, now what? Most people would answer in unison: You need to discover what you are passionate about, and that will direct you to your purpose. Do you think that is a true statement? Well, I think it depends on one's perspective. You can have a passion for something that is completely unconnected with your purpose. I love football, but I am quite sure that becoming a league player was never to be an outcome of my purpose.

If you are currently in a vacuous situation, fumbling around trying to batten down some form of personal identity and financial security, and you are having little to no luck in doing so, then perhaps it is time for a new line of thinking. Let's go back to square one. Your childhood . . . the one you had before you were socialized into proper behavior, when your imagination allowed you to see things that adults could not, and when you had no problem finding fun things to do all day long. Think of the things you liked to do before you grew up and adopted the universal concerns about money and status. Take your thinking a step further and consider those mental and physical activities that came easily to you and then . . . seriously consider that capabilities and talents are not present in a singular form—they are part of a particular intelligence.

In 1991, based on extensive research, renowned Harvard psychologist Howard Gardner identified seven distinct intelligences: visual-spatial, bodily-kinesthetic, musical, interpersonal, intrapersonal, linguistic, and logical-mathematical.[12] The interesting aspect of this research revealed that we have more than one "intelligence," and that each intelligence has a set of skill capabilities. For example, take the *visual-spatial intelligence*—this skill set includes capabilities in drawing, mapping, modeling, video producing, and multimedia interfacing, to name a few. These capabilities reflect an intelligent awareness of physical space, important for architects and sailors alike. Or, consider the *linguistic intelligence* that includes highly developed auditory skills and the ability to think in words, the ability to create various rhythms of prose and poetry, and the coveted ability to learn multiple languages quickly—a skill set that serves well the artist, the teacher, the writer, and the translators who worked in various critical roles of communications. Of course, we are familiar with the *logical-mathematical* intelligence that supports conceptual and abstract thinking, and the ability to recognize patterns and relationships—skills that are critical for scientists exploring the dark matter of space, scientists, and doctors studying new bacterium and viruses, and kids developing phone apps, and complex video games. For myself, I discovered early on that I enjoyed working with people to help those less fortunate. One of my intelligences is *interpersonal,* with the characteristics of empathy, understanding, and enjoyment, and empowerment when interacting with others. This bit of self-knowledge has been with

---

12Gardner, H. (2011). Frames of mind: The theory of multiple intelligences. (3ʳᵈ ed.). NY: Persus

I bring Gardner's description of the seven intelligences to the forefront of your quest. Allow yourself to return to your childhood way of thinking, so you utilize multiple central intelligences, and each intelligent field favors you with a skill set of multiple capabilities and talents. So, when you think back and remember that you used to love building things, or working on your tinker toy or erector creations, or filling the pages of your coloring books, or putting on plays for your parents, I want you to realize the inherent possibilities these fun activities held for your future career. I also want you to realize that your multiple intelligences endow you with *fields* of capabilities and talents that are interconnected, giving you, as an adult, a tremendous set of options for a career.

Our education systems have failed to support the broad range of capabilities and talents each of us have. In fact, the majority of individuals have no real idea of the range and complexity of their intelligences. According to Gardner, "we are all able to know the world through language, logical-mathematical analysis, spatial representation, musical thinking, the use of the body to solve problems or to make things, an understanding of other individuals, and an understanding of ourselves. Where individuals differ is in the strength of these intelligences - the so-called profile of intelligences -and in the ways in which such intelligences are invoked and combined to carry out different tasks, solve diverse problems, and progress in various domains" [underlining mine].

Our current education system operates on the assumption that everyone learns the same materials in the same way and that a universal testing system to measure student's learning progress is not only sufficient, but also optimal. Of course, it's not rocket science to realize that our educational system is heavily biased towards the linguistic and logical-quantitative modes of instruction and assessment. Unfortunately for the mass of students, there is little regard for the scope of capabilities and talents inherent in the different kinds of intelligences they possess and by extension, scant recognition of the individual ways through which they learn, remember, perform, and understand the world. Of course, what this means is by the time a student is ready to graduate high school, their ability to think has already been hijacked and squeezed into the tunnel- vision career choice they make in order align with correct decisions regarding their choice of college and major.

How many of you can say at some point in your primary schooling, you were individually tested to ascertain your natural talents and the scope of your capabilities? I know of a successful artist who has patrons around the world, yet she did not begin painting until she was in her mid-thirties. This twist of fate came about when she was hospitalized due to a nervous breakdown. One day in an effort to refocus her attention, her therapist coaxed her into trying her hand at painting. Astoundingly, her very first attempt produced a painting that could rival a Great Master's. No one was more surprised than she. How sad to think that such a talent had lain dormant all of those years.

Think also, of the new high school graduate who is ADHD and has determined he is going to be a brain surgeon. Or, how about the student who wants to become a motivational speaker, even though she is an introvert who is painfully shy? Seem ridiculous? Well, it is, but this kind career shopping happens. There is a reason why higher institutions of education have an advisement department: the majority of students have no clue as to neither their specific set of intelligences, nor their natural talents and capabilities. That's why it is that 50-70% of students change their major on an average of three times over the course of a four-year degree.

This is another example of the great disconnect between your childhood knowledge of yourself and what you loved to do versus the tunnel-vision perspective you developed in high school and how it can create a great void of uncertainty regarding your purpose in life? Worse still, one noticed how many passions have been relegated to the closets of wishful thinking and hung up as useless appendages, because they have no appropriate place in your collegiate or career plans?

In the grand journey of questing, throw down this gauntlet: Revisit your childhood and remember when you were a magical, creative creature whose imagination knew no boundaries, and your middle-school years where all kinds of possibilities filled your head, and your high school years when you were full of idealistic aspirations of how you could make a difference in the world. No quest could serve you better than this one.

CHAPTER 6

Passion: A Tool Every Quester Needs to Employ

Passions are the gales of life.
Alexander Pope, English poet

If you can't figure out your purpose, figure out your passion.
For your passion will lead you right into your purpose.
Bishop T. D. Jakes

The quest for purpose is marked along the way with signs of passion. For you to see these signs, you need your heart firmly seated within the realm of remembered possibilities. You should be like an excited child on a scavenger hunt and each remembrance of your imagination and dreams should be greeted with shouts of joy. You should be courageous and emboldened to change your story from one of self-limitation to one that remembers who you are, what talents you possess, things you are capable of, and what you deserve. You need to become reacquainted with your uniqueness and own it with boldness. We are here for a reason. Each of us has a seed of greatness that will sprout our unique blend of talents, wisdom, creativity, and courage of expression if we provide the water and light.

The first sign we should meet along our quest for self-data acquisition is one that reminds us to think BIG, to see the big picture of ourselves and our talents and capabilities. When we look at our wholeness, we can then perceive the recurring themes that created the patterns, which have guided our thoughts and behaviors as we have grown into adulthood. With a bird's-eye view, we are in a position to see the patterns that have continually emerged and we can evaluate their contribution to our lives. We might examine what types of people, what kinds of things, and what unique circumstances we are drawn to again and again. We might even examine those life experiences that were full of joy, and light, and wonder what special occurrences were at play. Themes and patterns are a particularly effective learning tool.

Just as a farmer tends his fields, it is up to us to tend to the harvest we have growing in our thoughts and actions. We need to become master cultivators and pruners. We need to take the usual questing questions and reframe them. The question: "what do you love about yourself?" should be reframed to ask: " What do you *not* love about yourself? When you reflect on this, allowing the answers come to you, then you are positioned to weed and prune where it will make a difference, leaving a nice clean field ready for re-cultivation in elements that are positive. Rather than asking, what is preventing you from exploring a possible career that you are passionate about, reframe the question to ask: What is supporting you in your exploration of a possible career that you are passionate about? The questing tools of re-storying and reframing bring about a seriously new level of clarity.

Questing: An Additive/Subtractive Paradigm

Passion, *passio*, refers to suffering in Latin and medieval French, whereby one is acted upon with emotions that are set apart from logic and reason. The term is a perfect fit for those on a quest in search of their purpose. One can have passion for something and yet, at the same time suffer from the yearning of passion when that something is unnamed and unfounded in their life. Passion is rooted in pleasure and in purpose. This is an important distinction to make. I have a passion for astronomy, yet I do not have the scientific/mathematical intelligence to pursue astronomy as a career. I also have a passion for music, but I have never considered music as a career or a life purpose; rather, it is a pursuit, something that brings me great joy and something that I would miss terribly if it were not a part of my life. I would feel as though my favorite color had been taken from my sight.

Passion is not evenly distributed between what one thinks, what one feels, and the actions behind what one does. One can have a great passion for horse racing and be very knowledgeable regarding particular horses, their owners and trainers, and the

40

jockeys who ride them—but that passion is far removed from the physical and mental profession of nurturing, training, and racing a horse to the Triple Crown. One is a pursuit of pleasure and the other is a pursuit of purpose. A passion of pleasure does not require great sacrifices, untold hours of focused discipline and hard work . . . or heartbreak when faced with devastating setbacks, as a passion of purpose does. On the other hand, a passion of pleasure will never experience the exhilarating joy of success that a passion of purpose delivers. A life's purpose has inestimable value and is therefore sacred; as such, the passionate pursuit of purpose becomes sacred also.

The quest of searching for your life's purpose is a demanding voyage. It requires your attention and the determination to embrace those passions in your life that are additive (even if you think they have weak currency career-wise) and to disengage from those passions (even when you are extremely fond of them) that do not serve your life and purpose (gambling, for example). The quester must be courageous and forge ahead to reach the Grail. That most certainly means that you will be required to leave some mindsets and behaviors, some environments, some circumstances, and above all, some people by the wayside.

Take for example, your family and clan members. Are you from a family of a long lineage of attorneys, or doctors, police officers, chefs, teachers, mechanics, etc.? Did you or do you now feel the heat to follow family tradition, especially when it is obvious to everyone who knows you that you have all the qualifications necessary to excel in the family profession? I know of an individual whose father pounded the kitchen counter with his fist when this person revealed he was majoring in theatre, with the intention of becoming a director. His father, turning a beet red with disbelief and anger, screamed, "Life isn't about the movies! You come from a long tradition of farmers. This farm, our home, has been in our family for five generations. You are the only son, it is your duty to bring your education back to the farm and continue looking after it. You need to seriously grow up!" I feel for this son, as this is a heavy burden to carry. It is very much a "no win" situation—if he leaves behind his passion for film and storytelling, there will be a vacancy in his soul his whole life long. Yet, if he turns his back on his family

41

and the family farm, he most likely will never be able to forgive himself. Imagine the guts one would need to walk away from a homestead that has been in the family for a hundred years.

You must also turn aside from those early childhood experiences that show up in your adult life as insecurities or barriers to your purpose. Perhaps, you witnessed a nasty divorce between your parents; perhaps, you have had to deal with the pressure to take sides, one parent against the other, or perhaps the divorce created a huge void in the home and in your life (a lot of emotions are locked into that experience and usually there are a lot of misperceptions that find their way into your adult perspectives). You need to separate the child's perceptions from reality, as no child has the mental and emotional capability to accurately understand the circumstances and trauma around divorce. Hence, children with a divorce consciousness, usually have self-esteem issues, blame issues, and a fear of getting emotionally close to someone. As an adult, the idea of marriage, becomes very black and white as they often exhibit strong, controlling behaviors. Many familial issues that a child will experience will distort their adult perspectives on a host of circumstances and situations. The act of restorying their childhood experiences is an excellent way to rewrite those pivotal experiences in adult terms.

The quest for purpose demands a clear focus on the wonderful talents and capabilities you arrived on the planet with, and when these are when coupled with adult life experiences, your purpose might rise like a phoenix from a situation that is, less than desirable. This would be my story, as I started my entrepreneurial endeavor by way of such an experience. The details are simple enough—I had engaged a professional to prepare my taxes. Unfortunately for me, he had not made note of all my deductions. When I brought this to his attention, he copped an attitude and suggested that, as I was already getting enough back, I should just let the unaccounted deductions go. My position was that I was entitled to the deductions, which he had been remiss in reporting and I wanted him to redo the forms and include those deductions. He wasn't very happy

42

with my demands and we went toe to toe over the situation. In the meantime, I made it a point to research the tax law, which I later put before him and demanded that he do my tax preparation according to the law. Although not happy with my aggressive approach, he begrudgingly redid my taxes. I thought about that situation for a long time, as the extra deductions meant a significant amount of financial return. I realized that had I not been so aggressive, I would not have received those deductions, and the "professional" I had engaged certainly wasn't working for my optimal benefit. I also considered that perhaps he wasn't up-to-date on the new tax laws, which was unfortunate, as this was his profession (and obviously not his purpose). It was from this experience that I saw an opening by which I could change my life and do something with purpose and value. Before this experience, I could not have envisioned that my years of practicing tax law would lead me to my purpose. This was a case where my logical, mathematical, reasoning, calculating intelligence merged with my interpersonal intelligence to create an opportunity where I could help people create financial awareness and prosperity. It was an additive dynamic, engaging both my passion for accounting and business entrepreneurship, and my purpose in teaching people how to manage their financial affairs.

By far, the most difficult aspect of being on a quest for your purpose, are the people you have to deal with. One has to be diligent in relationships, as people (even close friends) can bring you down with their negative viewpoints. This is especially true within the work environment, where people try to derail you, some of them with the most sincere of smiles. It seems there is phony, a down caster, a backstabber, and troublemaker reside in every office. It is up to you to be a conscious observer of how people respond to you and your ideas and actions. It is also up to you to filter out the negative thoughts, behaviors, and actions surrounding you daily. Of course, it is beneficial when you have a handle on the relationship dynamics going on in your workplace.

It is good to cultivate the finesse of a team leader, an arbitrator, a priest, and an angel—as long as you keep possession of your identity the one that has been forged by you and you alone.

The most needed companion for your quest journey is Faith--faith in yourself, your abilities, and your purpose. If you have lost faith, then you need to locate where you left it and make it your partner. Faith will bolster your confidence, like no other friend can. It will send your fears packing and require you to dwell in the magic of possibilities. It will push you to trust your instincts and it will remind you of your nascent dreams and the responsibility you have to take them seriously. Faith will encourage your mindfulness, sharpen your powers of observation, and ground you in your purpose, if you just let it. It will reveal the difference between a purpose and a profession. In the slightest of moments, faith will unveil a vision for your life. In return, faith will demand your transformation from a state of confusion to a state of enlightenment, from a state of depression to a state of joy and passion. Acceptance of t h i s is essential, only if you desire faith to be your companion on this journey.

CHAPTER 7

The Most Transformation Questing Tool of All: A Vision-Action Board

Cherish your visions and your dreams as they are the children of your soul,
the blueprints of your ultimate achievements.

Whatever your mind can conceive and believe,
the mind can achieve.

Napoleon Hill

Built on the above sage advice from Napoleon Hill, psychologists have found that the act of creating a vision-action board is an illuminating one. Stories abound of successful people like motivational speakers Jack Canfield and John Assaraf, actor and ex-governor Arnold Schwarzenegger, Oprah, author Wayne Dyer, Tiger Woods, and actor Jim Carey, to name a few from hundreds, that have praised the concept of a vision-action board. And, it's not just Hollywood and motivational celebrities that use them, Olympic athletes, television personalities, sport figures, and politicians have all started to share how vision-action boards have helped define and sustain their success. Vision-action boards help you to get clear about whom you are and what you want to achieve. The act of creating a personal vision-action board makes your dreams and goals more tangible and solid as you form an energetic bond to all that you plan to have and achieve. A vision-action board also acts in another important capacity—it is like a roadmap that provides you with direction when you take an impromptu side road and realize you're going in a wrong direction. When it's well done, it will become your guiding light, your North Star.

What does it mean . . . a vision-action board well done? To answer that, we need to return to our journey quest for our purpose. We will also need to understand the purpose of the vision-action board we choose to create. For example, a vision-action

45

board keeps your dreams and goals constantly in your sight and your mind. According to the amount of energy and passion you have towards your dreams and goals, the vision-action board will surround you with an even greater abundance of energy; keeping your energy high and your focus strong. It becomes well done when you have established a clear picture of what you want and that desire resonates in every cell of your person.

Motivational speaker Brian Tracey says, "An average person with average talent, ambition, and education, can outstrip the most brilliant genius in our society, if that person has clear, focused goals."

The partner component to goals is values. Whereas goals are specific locations on a map, values are the compass that keep us on purpose, and keep our principles intact. Goals reflect our purpose, values reflect our passion. There is profound wisdom to this, as sometimes goals don't make it, and we temporarily think we have failed at something we were striving for; however, because our goals are built on our values, we realize that the goal merely needed some tweaking. Goals that are based on values are living entities that collaborate with us in living and working with purpose. If you don't know what your values are, you know who you are. A vision-action board will help you with your quest in realizing your true self and your inherent purpose. With these components in place, your vision-action board is well done.

You also need a mission statement. The mission statement connects your passion with your purpose to manifest your dreams and the incremental goals to get you there. This is essential to have a well done vision-action board. To create a mission statement, it's important to ask the right questions. What would you like to be, do, or have in your life and your business if you knew you could have anything you wanted? If you really believed it was possible and you deserved it? If you did not fear failure? If you had the support you needed? If you had abundant financial resources and all the time you needed?" If you knew without a doubt that you could succeed . . . what would you love to do?

What would make your hands and feet happy, your intellect excited, and your spirit soar? You have the answer. Your consciousness has every answer to every question you can summon, regarding who you are and what your purpose in life is. The problem seems to be that by the time you have attained adulthood, your consciousness is deeply mired in the muck of societal conventionality. To find any answer to your identity and purpose, return to your childhood and reconnect with your dreams.

A properly constructed vision-action board is a creative mix of images that represent something you want to have, or a symbol of something you want to achieve. These images represent feelings that you would like to experience, people you would like to attract into your life, events you would like to attend, activities you would like to be a part of, excellent health, a wonderful, nurturing relationship, a coveted prize for excellence in your field, the outcome of a creative project, like a book . . . the possibilities are endless.

A well built vision-action board needs to reek of positivity, inspiration, and d i v i n e revelation. Your strengths should become apparent by the choice of images, the poetry, the scribbles of ideas on a napkin, the congratulatory wishes from friends on a successful project, the motivational sayings that you have plucked from magazines and books . . . images and words that have sincere meaning, which will reconnect you to your dreams and invest them with inspired action.

There are no constraints, other than your own personal limiting beliefs, for what you envision for your life, and the actions you desire to take to make your dreams come true. When you write your mission statement, post a current photo of yourself next to it to make the physical and mental connection. When you make a list of your lifestyle goals, surround them with travel postcards to create excitement for future vacations to special locations you have long dreamed of visiting. When you create your business plan, surround it with fake (but very realistic looking) thousand dollar bills.

Your money goals are an important aspect of your overall financial vision for yourself and your business. Don't be timid on this one! You may have to really stretch your limits for imagining financial abundance, especially in our current times, as all we have heard on a daily basis for the past decade is how bad the world economies are and how millions of people are out of work. While this is true, and we need to be sympathetic to those experiencing severe financial hardships, we also need to keep a realistic perspective on the negativity we are.

The purpose for your vision-action board, Napoleon Hill, who wrote the seminal prosperity book a century ago, Think and Grow Rich cautioned his readers that "It's not only about thinking, it's about believing." It's at this juncture that so many people get off path and become disillusioned with the process and purpose of creating a vision-action board. If you don't believe you can achieve something, your disbelief and negative thoughts will make sure you that you will not achieve it. Science, long ago, proved that like attracts like. Gandhi was an excellent mentor in understanding this. His advice, which translates into everyday living was: If you want peace, do not study war.

My advice is: If you want to discover your purpose, stop saying that you have no idea what your purpose is. If you want to envision success, stop complaining about the difficulty of getting ahead. Remember, you are what you eat . . . physically, intellectually, emotionally, and spiritually. It's really that simple.

Simply having a vision is not enough. Vision must be backed with imagination, determination, faith, hope, and passion. It must have purpose and a well thought-out plan of action. Your vision–action board can be considered well done, if it vetoes the limiting beliefs of your unconscious mind and supports without hesitation your dreams and aspirations. How can you distinguish between the two? Think of Don Quixote and his fight with the windmill. As he relayed the story, he realized there were two possible outcomes in his battle with the windmill.

48

Its wings could pitch him into the mud or fling him to the stars. Remember, you live in a polar universe. There are two sides to every possibility. Your limiting beliefs will drag you down like a wet blanket, while your belief in possibilities will soar your spirit to the clouds. That's how you tell the difference.

How to Recognize When You Have Reached Your Destination
and Found Your Purpose

- You see the theme and patterns of your life intermesh with humanity and the Universe. You realize your contribution is important.

- You feel at one with the world, everything is in its rightful place. Synchronicities become apparent and start to make sense, pointing you in the right direction.

- The right people with the right sources show up at exactly the right time to support your purpose.

- You feel as though your body is resonating at a higher frequency, that unseen hands are guiding you on your path.

- You see things more clearly, visually and mentally, as though a fog has lifted.

- A world of new and exciting ideas suddenly opens up to you and you have deep and insightful conversations with people you just met.

- You become intellectually hungry as you experience leaps of insight and gain a profound understanding of concepts and ideas that have heretofore passed by you unknown.

- You find yourself creating at an extraordinary level, well beyond your previous capacity. You feel as though a Muse is working through you.

- Time ceases to have the same importance as you become passionate about your work and find yourself surrounded by kindred spirits who are passionate about the same things as you.

- You are beyond happy . . . you are in a perpetual state of bliss.

- You have reunited the adult you with the child you and now you two are living and working in harmony. You have found your passion after a serious quest for your Holy Grail.

- You know you have found your purpose when you are excited every single day of your life. So excited, in fact, that you can hardly wait to jump into bed at night because you know the joy morning will bring.

- You have become a self-actualized individual.

CHAPTER 8

Legacy: Become a Leader

The work that calls you, inspires you, and turns you into a passionate self-actualized person . . . is Great Work.

OD Harris

Self-actualizing people tend to be spontaneous and creative; and not overly constrained by social conventions, according to Maslow. In his research, Maslow noticed that self-actualized individuals had a better grasp of reality, understood the complications and convolutions of business commerce were independent thinkers, and were very private when it came to their individual development regarding their potentialities and inner resources. Maslow also realized that the individuals he studied had similar personality traits. All were reality-centered and easily able to differentiate between what was fraudulent and what was genuine. They were also problem-centered, treating life's difficulties as problems that had solutions.

Most importantly, Maslow discovered that self-actualized individuals have moments of extraordinary "peak" experiences that present profound moments of love, understanding, happiness, or bliss, during which they feel more whole, more alive, more aware of truth, justice, harmony, goodness, etc. and more in touch with personal inspiration and possibility. These individuals have many such peak experiences, when states of "flow" reveal one's highest potential for personal development. Self-actualization then, is the process of becoming oneself, developing one's potential, achieving an awareness of one's identity, and crafting a life that reflects these personal accomplishments. That's key, understanding true self-actualization blooms from within an individual, rather than from external factors. And, it all begins with the little child whose bright eyes sparkle with self-possibility.

The self-actualized individual dreams big because they have faith in their God-given talents. They have a sense they exist right here, right now for a reason. I have never met an actualized individual with the mindset that their life, and everyone and everything in it, are simply random events occurring in a chaotic world. To the contrary, self-actualized individuals believe everyone is here with the purpose of contributing to humanity and the planet in an additive way. (We can only shake our heads in disbelief at how the world has veered so sharply off track.) For those of us that live in a free, democratic society, we should consider ourselves very fortunate. Our governments and corporate institutions may be more powerful than they should be, yet those of us who have put in the time to find and unlock our purpose have to admit, a laser-sharp concentration, with committed dedication and hard work still delivers opportunities for success. The circumstances necessary to grow a leader are all around us. All we have to do is to step up to the plate, declare ourselves in the game, play hard (and fair), share the credit with our team members, and give kudos to the fans who support us. Nevertheless, how do you know when you have truly become a leader? In my opinion, true leaders lead. They *WANT* to serve others. They *WANT* to support others in the realization of their dreams. They *WANT* to make a difference. They want to leave a legacy that records their successes, the fact that they were once here, and took their life's energy, their intelligence, their talents, and capabilities, and made a difference in the world.

If we strive to become a leader, if we want to make a difference in our organization, our community, or even the world on some level, we must set the example. We must demonstrate integrity in our person and in our work. We must persevere in difficult times and show ourselves to be someone worthy of followers. We make our mark as a leader by leading, by demonstrating an inspired purpose and an endearing passion that supports it. Passion and purpose are the posts that support great ideas; contribution is the lintel that creates the capstone. Together, they provide the gateway to success and legacy.

AFTERWARD

OD's Ten Principles by which to Live and Prosper

---

1. Realize what you do now, whom you love now, and what you study now all contribute to who you will become. Practice self-reflection and seek insight and wisdom. Check your goals against your purpose every now and then to make sure you are on track. More importantly, check your passion levels, as they are a direct indication of how your purpose is going.

2. Fine-tune your sense of self-awareness. Stay connected to your intelligences, talents, and capabilities. Develop a greater awareness of what's happening on in your community and in the world. Be sure to commit some portion of your time and resources towards making a positive difference.

3. Stay grounded and focused on becoming the best YOU. To know oneself and to love oneself is a gift of inestimable value. To realize and honor your purpose is the greatest contribution you will make to humanity.

4. Surround yourself with good people and make time for them. Those closest to you are often your best teachers and supporters. Be in the present when you are with them. Be concerned with their lives and goals and how you might be able to assist in their success. Be open to learn, as there is always something to learn from every person who comes into your life.

5. Release your prejudices and nurture non-judgmental acceptance. Release anyone or anything that brings negativity into your life. Expect and embrace conflict—it's part and parcel of working together in collaboration. Conflict is a great supporter of creative idea-exchange.

6. Be creative and curious. Be open to change. Expect, even welcome the unexpected, as it arrives to help you sharpen your focus and greater define your purpose. Ask lots of questions and clear your mind enough to hear the answers--they are road signs illuminating the path to your destiny.

7. Learn from your mistakes. Don't regret them or berate yourself for making them. Change your perspective and see mistakes as really good friends that will teach you invaluable lessons if you are willing to learn. Edison remarked that mistakes are the quickest and surest route to success.

8. Always search for people and things that are highly motivating. They can be found anywhere . . . next door, at the cinema, in a nursing home, a TV or book biography, and a dozen other places. Develop your radar signal for motivational experiences.

9. Fill your purpose with overflowing passion. Cultivate it and take care to nurture it like you would a God-given, one-of-a-kind prized possession, which it is.

10. . Have no regrets! Let go of the "shoulda, coulda, woulda" defeatist thinking that serves no purpose. Be good to yourself, learn from your choices, and honor the possibilities that slipped away. When you are on purpose, possibilities are like stars—too numerous to count, and opportunities abound, usually in circumstances you would not have dreamed of. Learn the art of appreciation and give thanks for everyday for your life's abundance in all things.

A possibility is a hint from God. One must follow it.
Sören Kierkegaard

FOOTNOTE REFERENCES

Arnett, J. (2004). Emerging Adulthood: The Winding Road from the Late Teens through the Twenties. MA: Clark University.

Brinthaupt, T. & Lipka, R. (Eds.) (2002). Understanding early adolescent self and identity: An introduction. NY: SunyPress.

Gardner, H. (2011). Frames of mind: The theory of multipleintelligences. (3rd ed.). NY: Persus.

Henseler, C. (Ed.) (2012). Generation X goes global: Mapping a youth culture in motion. NY: Routledge.

Jabr, F. (2012). The neuroscience of 20-somethings. *Scientific American.*

Marcia, J. E., (1966). Development and validation of ego identity status. *Journal of Personality and Social Psychology.*

Maslow, A. (1998). Toward a psychology of being. (3rd ed.). NY: Wiley, 1998.

Robinson, K. (2013). Finding your element: How to discover your talents and passions and transform your life. Viking: USA.

Tulgan, B. (2009). Not everyone gets a trophy: Managing Generation Y. MA: Jossey- Bass.

Winograd, M. & Hais, M. (2012). Why Generation X is sparking a Renaissance in entrepreneurship. *Inkadescent—Ezine for Entrepreneurs.*